QUANTUM THEORY FOR CATS

Ian Stuart was born in Lancashire in 1945, and has lived in Leeds, Manchester, Derbyshire and on the Isle of Man. After thirty years in the teaching profession, he now works as a Ghost Trail Guide in York. His poems have been widely published in Yorkshire-based journals and magazines, but this is the first book with his name on the front cover.

Quantum Theory
for Cats

IAN STUART

Valley Press

First published in 2017 by Valley Press
Woodend, The Crescent, Scarborough, YO11 2PW
www.valleypressuk.com

First edition, first printing (November 2017)

ISBN 978-1-908853-90-5
Cat. no. VP0107

A CIP record for this book is available from the British Library.

Cover illustration by Ben Hardaker.
Cover and text design by Jamie McGarry.

Printed and bound in Great Britain by
Imprint Digital, Upton Pyne, Exeter.

Contents

for Ann
with love

Quantum Theory for Cats

I am Schrödinger's cat.
From time to time
he opens the box
and there I am
or not.

Am I alive or dead?
I'm a bit hazy on that one...

I can come and go as I please –
visit my friend Macavity
or pass time with cousin Smiler
who sometimes lives in Cheshire
and sometimes doesn't.
Me? I'm in and out all the time.
Now and where, here and when.

Notice he chose *me* for his experiment
and not Schrödinger's dog.
That would have put quantum physics back
a hundred years.

2.

I am Schrödinger's dog.
I love you.
Give us a biscuit.
I've just shat on your lawn.

In Waterstones

between Economics
and European History,
a woman is weeping
silently
because bookshops,
like empty churches
and doctors' waiting rooms,
are holy places
and to be respected.

Face buried in her hands
she stands, convulsed
by grief too real
for this warm place
humming with words.

A boy in a red shirt,
tidying shelves, looks up,
walks over. She clings to him,
staining his red shirt
with her polite tears.

Shaving

Each morning I become my father, shaving.

The foam can farts a slug of gel into my palm.
I fluff it to a fog which shrouds
the landscape, flattens all the hills and valleys,
leaving nothing but my nose, which stands
proud, like a mountain ridge above the mist.

I start the first stroke under my left ear
along the jaw and up the other side.
He did it that way too. Then down
the face in stripes, just like a neat clipped lawn,
always making sure there are no tufts
or clumps which might escape the gliding blade.
Lastly that triangle round the mouth
with all those creases, all those indentations.

That's it. We're done. I wipe the mirror clean.
The fog has cleared. I look up, and he's there –
the deep-set eyes, the thinning silver hair.
We nod our usual greeting, turn away
to face the business of another day.

British Summer Time

That last pretence of summer –
slanting sunlight, and the air
settling into velvet – has gone.

Street lamps stutter,
pour their pools of steely light
and photoflash each passing face
before it fades into shadow.

We turn back the clocks
enjoying, for a moment, the conceit
that we can turn back time,
control that slippery, elusive hour
which we have lost
or maybe not yet lived.

999

You often see the ambulance round here
(the population's getting old)
and things happen – usually at night.

You see their headlights swing into our road,
moving slowly till they find the house.
They go in quietly, without a fuss.

Ten minutes later and they're out.
Wheelchair or stretcher? You can guess
how serious it is. Doors thump shut.

I close the curtain.

It will come to all of us at last –
the pain that gnaws and can't be talked away,
the bloodied sheet, the sudden, unexpected
loss of self.

I wonder, when my turn comes,
if my neighbour, peeking through his blind,
will find some pity for me
within the selfish joy of his reprieve.

Icarus

I came too late
and never saw his face,
just a shrouded figure on the stretcher
and boots protruding from the plastic sheet.

A summer afternoon. The sun lay
like a warm hand on his back
as he climbed up to fix a broken tile.
He could see for miles from here –
the hills as soft as smoke,
the sea air prickling like champagne.

Reaching for his tools
he trod on air,
saw the sky slide sideways,
heard the seagull's scream
cut

Just the boots
the sort you wear for doing outside work,
clarted with dried mud
and the left one's lace undone.

Saint 1

Illumination only came through effort –
the parchment scraped, the pigments
ground and mixed with oil,
the whole design approved
before he tipped a brush
with liquid sky to start the toil.

And then the interruptions –
for chapel, labour in the fields,
the lack of good light, the winter mornings
his fingers wouldn't work for the sly cold,
the unforgiving, empty horizon.

He did the best of it
half-waking, eyes clenched
against the bleaching light.

A kind of holy absence
fell on him, and at the end,
when the bell woke him for chapel,
a tiny angel stood there on the page
with yellow gown and silver halo
the size of a nail paring.

Years later, blind, irritable,
waiting impatiently for death,
the angel came again
in a robe the colour of sunlight,
and behind his head
the crescent moon.

Saint 2

Saint or madman?
Maybe both. He looked the part –
hair greasy as a fat ewe's back –
eyes damson-dark behind a fall of beard.

Lived in a shoulder-high stone shed
he built with slates and stuff he found
dumped by the tide in straggling drifts of weed.

Ate barnacles and whelks scraped off the rocks,
and rabbits which he blessed before
he stretched their necks and skinned them
with a flint the Old Ones left behind.

He had the healer's touch –
would cure a winter fever
by rubbing spittle on the eyes and mouth.

Always praying.
Ploughmen heard him in the early dawn,
bawling at the sky and giving God
a good lambasting.

Longliners in the bay at night
heard his voice – a trumpet call.
Naked, waist-deep in the slopping waves
he sang the mackerel in.

It worked, too.
Every boat came back
loaded with twitching silver
those times he sang.

One autumn night the sky was filled with fire –
islands of emerald in a sapphire sea
turning and shifting above our heads.
The air crackled like autumn ice.

Next day we found him dead among the dunes.
Flat on his back, eyes open wide.
They say he died of wonder.

To bury him seemed wrong and so
we left him for the gulls to pick at.

When they were done
we each took something from him –
a tooth, an ankle bone
for a memory

and left the wind
to draw a sheet of sand
over the rest.

The Poets

This man could give a voice to stones,
cause trees to shriek in a December gale,
see through warm flesh down to the bone,
make houses creak, and ancient timbers fail.

This woman annotates her pulsing blood
and makes it roar again in others' veins.
She pleads the possibility of good
and, dying, leaves that rhythm in our brains.

These are the poets, vilified and cursed,
who wear their souls turned inside out
and lead us, struggling, to face the worst –
where faith is sin, the only virtue doubt.

The New Rembrandt

Using complex data sampling, a Dutch computer firm
recently created a new composite Rembrandt portrait.

A tradesman shopkeeper perhaps,
stylish in his Sunday best –
the ruff starched crisp and white.
A countenance so everyday,
so commonplace, and yet a palimpsest
of all the people he has ever been
from boy to man.

Truth lies in that face.

He is a phantasm, a chimera,
a million data points distilled,
a clever magic trick.

Or maybe there's a ghost in the machine,
a bug which emulates the human soul,
an Instant Message flashed up on the screen,
a spark of hope which makes the broken whole.

Cézanne

He stands before the empty canvas, sees
sky, fragile and faultless as a blown bubble,
a sea of crinkled cellophane
and a long, lost summer afternoon
smelling of grass, warm stone
and pine needles.

Sunlight shifts and flickers,
dappling cottage walls
as the trees nod in agreement
with the warm wind.

A path leads down past ragged outcrops
to the town, where roofs glow oven-hot,
and cats lie stunned in alleyways
flat as their own shadow.

I stand before the picture, watching
it fade into the frame.
Footsteps. The gallery is closing.

Outside the air is sharp with rain
and petrol smells. I am immune.
My sky is blue and endless, and my soul
warmed by a distant sun.

Venice Morning

Rocked in the slack
water between sleep and waking,
she stretches in the bed,
brushes one soft fallen lock
from her cheek,
breathes lavender and musk, and sweat.
Her eyelids tremble open.

A tide of sunlight spills across one wall –
painted cherubs in a net of gold,
and soaks the carpet, strewn
with rumpled stockings, underslips and lace.

Outside, the city reinvents itself
in slapping water, footsteps,
and the wash of passing boats. She slips

from the bed, steps silently,
dressed in light, to the window
where her lover waits, whispering his passion.
Breathing in his words, she shivers.

The morning sunshine prickles her skin.

She turns back to the room,
grabs the filmy gauzes, the brocades,
gathering them around her like a cloud
and is gone with him,
her footsteps fading in the busy street.

Venice Evening

An apricot light beyond the open windows,
the smell of perfume, rosin, sweat.
Heels click back and forth
on a wooden floor, chairs scrape.
The swaying cello sheds notes, heavy
as the drops hanging in her ears,
soft as her powdered cheek.

Marsala in a Venetian glass; starched petticoats
and clever fingers sliding curtain rings.

And after,
waking to feel her breath against my skin,
her tiny movements, like a sleeping cat.

Outside, black water laps the landing stage;
footsteps, quiet curses, the splash of oars.
Musicians going home, and she with them.

The pattering of rats behind the plaster.

A dog howls in the shadowed courtyard.

Beyond the window,
dawn pales like a bruise.

In Transit

They are everywhere,
the pre-born;
housed in round
bellies, breathing
their own ocean,
stretching, kicking
in the cushioned dark.

Water turns to
bone, gels
to flesh fed
by the red roar
in their veins.

And ripe, they fall
into a welter of blood and light.
Travellers arriving
at the wrong destination,
bawling their anger.

Lost Child

Assembled from the diaries of John Evelyn, 1620-1706

A long frost and a deep snow.
This had been the severest winter
any man alive had known in England.
Crows' feet were frozen on their prey;
islands of ice enclosed both fish and fowl.

My dear boy fell in such a fever
naught could bring him comfort or relief.

Whilst there was still life in him
we sent to London for physicians.
The river froze; the coach broke down
ere it had gone a mile beyond our gates.

All artificial help failing, he died.

I caused his body to be lapped in lead.
We buried him next night in Deptford church

and all my joy of life with him.

Jane Nightwork

Flat on my back
in the black grass,
daisies, like fallen stars
about my face,
and his hand
up my petticoats
and heading slowly north.

We haven't got all night.

I am his first time.

He is fifteen.

Our clothes fall, rustling, to the ground
and he is on me, gasping, urgent,
shivering between fear and lust.
My fingers skim his chest, feel
the soft skin, the beating heart beneath.

Flat on my back
in the black grass,
open as earth
and he the plowman.

Afterwards he wept – they often do
that first time, then
I kissed away his tears
and we danced again.

Underneath his cloak we lay
and watched the circling stars until
dizzy with their reeling,
we slept.

When we woke
the moon had tilted, tipped
her bowl of light
so the air shimmered,
each field spiked with frost,
and the river slithered sleek
as quicksilver
through the sooty dark.

We dressed, backs turned
and took separate ways,
each nursing our delight, and shame,
like Eve and Adam
that first night in Eden.

Phone Call

'Do you remember, years ago,' he said,
'we met up in some bookshop. I was with
my sister. She was quite impressed with you –
said you had a gentleness, an air
of understanding – and a lovely voice.'

'That's nice,' I said, yet knowing as I spoke
I had no memory of that day at all.
It wasn't me they'd met.

The conversation ended, but he stayed,
my doppelganger – kindly, gentle, calm –
the kind of man I once hoped I'd become.

I look for him each morning in the mirror
and sometimes catch a glimpse,
but then he's gone.

Poetry for Birds

A pair of shelducks
pack the gusts tight
under their muscled wings.

Swallows write their own,
scrawling it with pen nib tails
on a sky edged with evening.

The clockwork lark
climbs its ladder of air,
sings until the spring
winds down
but sinking, leaves the song
still hovering there.

Afterwards

After the orgy was over
they lay, emission impossible,
in a heap together, like broken dolls.

One of them got to his feet.
'My bus will be here in a minute,'
he said, and started to look for his pants.

They unravelled themselves with some care,
leg from crotch, lip from nipple or thigh,
and fumbled with discarded clothing.
'Are these your knickers? So pretty!'
'Has anyone seen my tie?'

They said their goodbyes in the hallway,
where the cameraman clutched his equipment.
'That was fun. We must do it again.'
'Is there anyone needing a lift?'

The door closed softly behind them.

I went back and plumped up the cushions,
got some Vanish for stains on the chairs,
put fresh batteries in my vibrator,
and, smiling, slipped quickly upstairs.

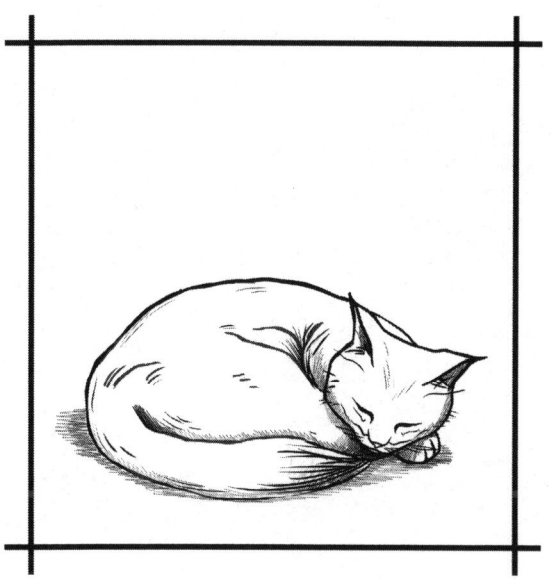

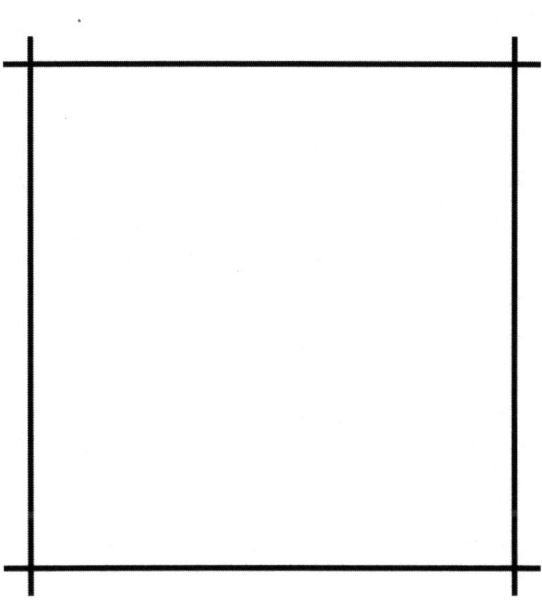